H. H. HOLMES

THE HORRIFIC TRUE CRIME
STORY OF A MURDEROUS DOCTOR

JEFFREY PATTERSON

Table of Contents

Introduction

H. Holmes holds an important and unique spot in America's history. He came to be known as the country's first known serial killer. Prior to his run of murders, there hadn't been anyone regarded as a notorious killer of this kind in the United States.

One of the more interesting parts to the story of this intelligent, yet sadistic doctor, is there are pieces of the puzzle that just don't quite fit together. Throughout this incredible tale, there are mysterious inconsistencies between some of the confessions Dr. Holmes made about people he'd murdered and what was actually proven to be true. It's a story that is baffling and troublesome, but incredibly intriguing.

There are also differing accounts about the infamous "Murder Castle," as it came to be known. While it's not the only place Holmes did his torturing and killing, it is the location where he took the lives of many of his victims. The various schools of thought aren't about whether or not he killed people there. Mostly the debates are over the purpose of the huge building, along with what kind of secrets the building enclosed. Some people believe there were hidden passageways, trapdoors, and other enigmatic features Holmes used to toy with his victims before eventually killing them.

This book will also explore the theory that Dr. H. H. Holmes is actually the true killer of a number of prostitutes in London. There are those who believe that Holmes was, in fact, "Jack the Ripper."

This is a story that dates back to the late 19th century. It's one filled with fraud, trickery, torture, and death. It has twists and turns, mysteries, and conviction. And when it appears to come to a close, things might not quite be what they seem.

This is the story of America's first known serial killer, Dr. H. H. Holmes.

Chapter 1

Herman Webster Mudgett

May 16, 1861, Herman Webster Mudgett was born to mother, Theodate Page Price, and father, Levi Horton Mudgett, in Gilmanton, New Hampshire. His existence in the world would eventually prove to be a curse of sorts for many who would come to cross paths with him. But, that wouldn't be discovered, of course, until a bit later in his lifetime when he would be known as Dr. H. H. Holmes.

Mudgett's family was quite wealthy. He grew up not wanting for much. His father came from a long line of farmers, and he worked in farming too, along with painting houses and as a trader.

It has been said by some that when Mudgett was a young boy he was abused by his father, suffering physical violence. There are also speculated accounts of his being bullied by kids at school and in the neighborhood. Differences of opinions exist about whether any of it is true.

Though nothing has ever surfaced that proves Mudgett was picked on or abused by anyone, his father was said to have been an alcoholic who was violent with all of the Mudgett family members.

As for the bullies at school, it is believed his peers picked on him because of his extreme intelligence. He did exceedingly well in school so his classmates thought him to be odd and arrogant. There were attempts by other kids to "put him in his place" and break him down.

In one alleged incident, a group of students wanted to scare Mudgett. They made him stand in front of a skeleton looking it in the face. They then put its hands on either side of his face to really frighten him. This reportedly scared, but later this incident would be credited for escalating his obsession with mutilation and death to a whole new level, as well as curing him of his fear.

Other stories have been told of Mudgett trapping small animals and then torturing them before eventually taking their lives. It may, or may not, be true. There are certainly those who believe these accounts could have come out of society's need to profile serial killers and fit them into a category to make sense of what they've done.

Another speculation was made about Mudgett's teen or early adult years. There were a couple of versions of this story. One was that he murdered a childhood playmate. The other, which is much more likely to have been something that happened, was that he may have killed a little boy before any of his known killings occurred. The suspicion arose from a story about a little boy who had disappeared in Mooers Forks, New York. It was reported by an eyewitness that the boy had been seen with Mudgett prior to his disappearance.

While questions were asked of him, Mudgett simply stated the boy had gone home to Massachusetts. That must have satisfied any curiosity at the time because there was never an investigation into what happened to the little boy. Mudgett ended up leaving town after that, which kept anything further from developing.

Mudgett was the middle child in a family of five children. From a very early age, he showed a high level of intelligence. He also had an extremely keen interest in medicine and medical practices, with an especially prudent eye toward dissection and mutilation of the human body.

High school graduation came in 1877 when Mudgett was 16 years old. He was still in Gilmanton at the time, but quickly moved to Alton to work in teaching. Alton is where adult life began for Mudgett.

ADULT LIFE

In the summer of 1878, Mudgett married his first wife, Clara A. Lovering. Less than two years into the marriage, the couple had a baby boy and named him Robert Lovering Mudgett.

During this time with Lovering, Mudgett enrolled in college at the University of Vermont located in Burlington, Vermont. He was 18 years old at the time. He would only stay for one year because he didn't like the school.

Mudgett had always had that strong pull toward medicine. It was still with him in his college-age years. He decided to go into the Department of Medicine and Surgery at the University of Michigan in 1882. He was a mediocre student during his time at the university and worked as an assistant to Professor Herdman in the anatomy lab.

One of the most notable things people would come to remember Mudgett for, as Holmes, was his methods of murder because there was often some type of torturous dissection involved. His school years working under Professor Herdman, the senior anatomy teacher, coupled with an earlier apprenticeship he held serving Dr. Nahum Wight back in New Hampshire, is likely when and where Mudgett learned much of what he used on his victims during their dramatic killings.

Throughout his time at the University of Michigan, Mudgett had access to numerous cadavers. He would steal the bodies, mutilate them and remove organs, and then use them to make money through insurance scams and the selling of body parts.

Around the time Mudgett was to graduate from the University of Michigan, his wife, Lovering, decided to leave Michigan and move back to New Hampshire to get away from him. Those who knew the couple personally reported there was domestic violence within the marriage. Witnesses had seen Mudgett abuse Lovering during their time together.

Not long after the couple's separation, Mudgett graduated from college. That didn't come without drama either, however. Graduation almost didn't happen for him because of a scorned hairdresser who'd been once widowed. She accused Mudgett of having lied by falsely promising to wed her. The situation was smoothed over in time, though, and Mudgett graduated from the University of Michigan in 1884.

Sometime after his graduation, Mudgett moved to Philadelphia to look for work. He took a job at Norristown State Hospital working as a keeper. It was a psychiatric facility that had only recently been established to keep patients from having to be transported so far away to another part of the state. He only worked there for a few days because he didn't find it suitable and decided to quit.

Mudgett didn't truly feel the need for employment. He was always swindling and hustling, conning whoever he could out of whatever money or property they had. He was a fraudster of many sorts, including eventually a bigamist. His jobs were often good resources for finding his targets for scams—some of his favorites being insurance schemes. At the peak of his career he was a pharmacist. It was a job that may have come to him as a result of a con.

After Mudgett left the job at the psychiatric hospital, he found another position in Philadelphia at a drugstore. Though he kept the job for longer, he would leave there also, when a story surfaced about a customer's son who died after taking medicine bought at the drugstore.

Mudgett, again, claimed he had nothing to do with the death of this boy. That didn't stop him from quitting his job and leaving the city, however. He decided his time was up in Pennsylvania soon after that. A change of scenery was due.

Chapter 2

The Emergence of H. H. Holmes

The drugstore debacle in Philadelphia left Mudgett feeling paranoid about the mounting evidence that could be piling up around him. Per that paranoia, he decided to move to a whole new state. He set his sights on Chicago, Illinois for his next venture. Before moving there, though, he made another decision to change his name.

There was a long line full of scams and fraud trailing along behind Mudgett. He didn't want to risk exposing himself in any way to victims of his past schemes or have any of his crimes catch up to him, so he changed his name. His new name came to be Henry Howard Holmes, or Dr. H. H. Holmes as he's known to most today.

By the second half of 1886, Holmes was living in Chicago. While exploring his new environment, he happened upon a pharmacy that was owned by the Holtons. It was located in the Englewood neighborhood of the city and Holmes quickly set forth on a path to infiltrate the corner drugstore with what was very likely a plan to take the business over for himself.

He was offered a job in the pharmacy and proved himself to be a good employee by all counts. He developed a good working relationship with Dr. Holton, who had also attended school at the University of Michigan, and his wife, Elizabeth. Eventually, Holmes bought the pharmacy from the Holtons, though it's also been speculated that he somehow swindled the couple out of their business and took it over as his own.

Later, rumors would also circulate that Holmes murdered both of the Holtons. That story was put to rest at some point when it was proven that the couple continued their lives into the 20th century still living in the Englewood neighborhood.

THE FRAUD CONTINUES

At the end of 1886, Holmes traveled to Minneapolis and married his second wife, Myrta Z. Belknap. Though he had been separated from Lovering, his first wife, for two years, he was still legally married to her at the time of his wedding to Belknap.

A couple of weeks after their wedding, Holmes filed for divorce from Lovering. He cited infidelity on her part as the reason for the dissolution of marriage. As there was no proof of the alleged behavior he was accusing Lovering of having committed, his case didn't proceed. This resulted in a bigamous marriage with his new wife, Myrta Belknap.

It's unclear if Belknap had any knowledge of Holmes' continuing marriage to Lovering. Regardless of her awareness, Belknap moved to Illinois to live with her husband in Wilmette, not far from Chicago. Later down the line, Holmes and Belknap had a daughter together and named her Lucy Theodate Holmes. She was born in July 1889 in Chicago.

Life in Chicago would prove to be quite rich for Holmes. The pharmacy turned out to be the perfect breeding ground for numerous scams that would pay off for the young doctor. One of his money-making schemes was based in forcing employees to carry life insurance policies and having his name added to them as a beneficiary. The scam would move on with Holmes eventually killing the benefactor employee, then receiving the insurance money.

The scam often wouldn't end there, though. He would then collect even more money by selling his victims' bodies to medical schools for research in the local area.

Not even a year after moving to Chicago, Holmes also invested in some real estate with plans for another scheme, or schemes as it would turn out. He purchased the lot that was on the corner directly across from his newly acquired drugstore. That lot was empty, but Holmes had no intention of leaving it that way.

Holmes told city officials and the builders he hired for the construction of his plans, which were to include some retail shops on the first floor, with one space being a new pharmacy to house his existing business, and the second floor to consist of several apartments.

Construction got underway in 1887. It wouldn't be long, though, before things would get complicated for everyone involved.

Holmes' vision of the building he wanted constructed on the large lot he purchased was one with three stories that he referred to as "The Castle." The original version of it only had the first two stories. The third floor, which was to function as a hotel, was never fully completed.

Dr. Holmes may have intended for his castle to be used as a hunting ground for cornering his victims from the very beginning. There have been countless accounts of odd features that were included on the inside of the building. Holmes' own story, however, was that the building was being established as a new location for his pharmacy, a useful addition for serving the community, and as a hotel to accommodate visitors coming to town for the World's Columbian Exposition planned for 1893. The expo was to serve as a 400th year celebration of Columbus' discovery of the Americas, which was expected to bring potentially millions of visitors to the area.

As the project got underway, the building and its intended uses were pretty much a mystery to many of the people involved in the construction process. The reason was because Holmes hired multiple contractors and different companies to keep things as confusing and unclear as he could. He didn't want any one person to have full knowledge of everything going into the building.

By keeping anyone from seeing the project in its entirety, he thought that no one would really understand its purpose. Sometimes he would start to get paranoid about contractors he felt saw too much. He would simply fire them and replace them with brand new workers.

About a year into the construction process, some of the hired engineers and architects were due payment. Holmes outright refused to pay. He did the same to the steel company he had brought in on the project, Aetna Iron and Steel. All of them brought lawsuits against him, accusing him of scamming them out of money.

Holmes also ordered a large amount of furniture since he would be housing a hotel on one floor of the building and apartments on another. When the pieces would arrive, he would move them into parts of the building that were hidden or closed off. Then he would put on an act as if the furniture was never delivered. As there was no furniture to be seen, he withheld payment. The furniture suppliers couldn't prove otherwise so they were never paid anything.

"The Castle" took around 4 to 5 years to be mostly completed. Its useful life would end up being quite short, but what happened within the walls of Holmes' newly built property has been the subject of story after story that has been passed forward through history and still lives on today.

Chapter 3

The Murder Castle

H. H. Holmes knew there would be a World's Fair held in Chicago in 1893. It had been planned for quite some time when he bought the empty lot across the street from the drugstore he had acquired. The Expo was to be a commemoration and celebration of Christopher Columbus' discovery of the Americas, but Holmes most certainly saw it as an opportunity for himself.

For that reason, many historians are certain Holmes was planning to use his new property as a murderous playground where he could lure people, toy with victims, torture them, and then finally kill them, making money off the bodies much of the time, too. It also gave him somewhere to hide and destroy evidence.

There are various stories about what secrets Holmes' building held. Claims have been found about hallways that wandered through the building in a maze-like fashion meant to confuse visitors so they'd be trapped. Many of the hallways, as well as staircases, reportedly went nowhere. They would simply stop at a dead end.

The original blueprints for the massive project showed there were 100 rooms inside with no windows. The building had two huge furnaces, but also an incinerator in the basement. There were chutes going from all of the floors above ground all the way down to the basement where the incinerator was. While those kind of chutes were normal in building's of that time, these chutes were larger than normal. Holmes' shoots were body-sized. The plans also indicated 51 doorways that curiously lead only to brick walls.

Some of the other notable features people have claimed were inside, what the public eventually deemed as the "Murder Castle," were rooms with soundproofing and some that were entirely airtight. Huge vats of acid were discovered in the basement, along with a crematorium, which was where the incinerator was located. Next to the incinerator, there were surgical tables and instruments like those found in operating rooms. Holmes' special interest in dissection was evident by the items uncovered inside his building.

When the building opened to the public, some shops did set up business on the first floor and had their own storefronts. The second floor was where Holmes did much of his torturing and killing. That belief is based on what was found on the second floor during a later investigation that would lead to Holmes' arrest.

The second floor was chocked full of all kinds of features that lead the authorities and the public to the shocking realization that Dr. Holmes was someone they did not want living in their community. Investigators and the police found there were all sorts of false walls and hidden passages where hinged segments could be folded to the side allowing for entry into other rooms without being detected.

One of the most disturbing discoveries were rooms that appeared to be used as gas chambers. The police found gas pipelines leading into rooms that were airtight. People trapped in those rooms would die of asphyxiation when gas was pumped into the room.

Holmes' "Murder Castle" is something that has been debated and studied by many for a long time. In the era in which it existed, sensationalist reporting was largely popular. Historians argue about whether the reports and various claims about the building were exaggerated. It was a common practice to embellish stories in that time to attract more readers. Shock and awe of the audience was the goal.

Some of what was said to be uncovered about the "Murder Castle" came from an investigation that was held when Holmes was away from the building. Suspicions had been mounting about what was rumored to be going on inside the World's Fair hotel. The police supposedly found many strange features that lead them to believe Holmes was torturing and murdering guests of the hotel—even using the hotel as his means of choosing his victims.

Apparently, news of the investigation and what was discovered made it to the investors Holmes had secured for the completion of the project. All of the investors pulled out leaving the third floor unfinished.

In the end, after Holmes' arrest, the "Murder Castle" went up in flames. Though no one was ever charged with starting the fire, it was believed that an arsonist set it. There were eyewitness reports of two men entering the building and then exiting a short time later. Not long after that, the whole thing caught fire. Accounts of a gas can found underneath the staircase at the back of the building were reported as well.

Eventually the building was restored where the "Murder Castle" had been. It housed a United States Post Office. In the late 1930s, that building was demolished. Another was built in its place. It remains a federal post office serving the Englewood community still today.

CARETAKER QUINLAN

There had been a caretaker hired by Holmes who had worked in his building during the years leading up to the World's Fair and after. His name was Patrick Quinlan. His job was to clean, do maintenance, and provide general upkeep for Holmes' hotel.

Due to his close association with Holmes and the "Murder Castle," Quinlan was suspected by some to have had involvement in some of the killings for which Holmes was being blamed. He was questioned about what he knew of the serial killer's antics from his time spent as caretaker of the building.

Quinlan was able to prove he was innocent and had no knowledge of what was happening in the building. He stated he was only an employee of Holmes, not an accomplice. His closest involvement with anything having to do with the victims of his employer's schemes was in having helped to build some of the trap doors leading into the rooms where he may have held them. He also admitted to helping line some of the rooms with asbestos meant for the dampening of sound. Quinlan maintained that even though he helped construct some of the strange mechanisms and features of the rooms where Holmes, almost certainly, killed people, he was unaware of their intended purposes. His innocence was accepted by authorities and Quinlan was never charged with anything.

In 1914, Caretaker Quinlan was found dead in his bedroom. His death was the result of suicide. He had poisoned himself by taking strychnine. Beside him, there was a note that read simply, "I couldn't sleep."

Friends of Quinlan said he was haunted for 19 years after witnessing what he had within the walls of Holmes' "Murder Castle." He hadn't slept in such a very long time that he just couldn't bear to keep living. They said Quinlan had spoken about being haunted in his dreams and that he would startle awake to even more hallucinations. He would call out for someone to help him. He was a man without peace.

With Quinlan's death went all the secrets that were held inside the Holmes castle. Historians and others who wanted to know what was housed within the walls of the huge hotel knew they'd have to accept they would probably never find out.

Consideration has to be given to the reason Quinlan killed himself, though. He claimed to be haunted every night for 19 years. He had also confessed to having constructed pieces of the hotel that had been reported on by what was called sensationalist media, both at the time and by present day researchers. One has to ask himself, why was this man unable to sleep? What was it he couldn't un-see, couldn't un-hear from his time working in that building? The haunting of Quinlan, which lead him to commit suicide, seems to point toward the Holmes hotel being more like the house of horrors it had been painted as by the media than what some would like to believe.

Chapter 4

The Murders

The exact number of murders H. H. Holmes committed is unknown. The range of what people believe to be the number of victims he had is incredible. It starts as low as just 2 and goes upwards of 200 on the other end.

One of the reasons it's so hard for historians to pin down the actual number has to do with Holmes himself. He did his best to elude the police for a very long time so he wouldn't have to own up to his crimes, and so he could continue to satisfy his cravings for mutilating and murdering humans while making money doing it. Eventually it did all catch up to him, though, and he confessed to killing 27 people. Shouldn't that be the end of it then?

One would think, but it was later discovered that some of the people Holmes confessed to killing were still very much alive, and even well. It was baffling to the police, but they did find some proof of some of the murders so there would be a conviction anyway. It never got any easier to figure out the number because, even while Holmes was in the gallows, he uttered another confession, stating he had actually only ever killed two people.

In any case, what is known is that Holmes was responsible for the murders of some people. The following are accounts of what has been uncovered about some of this serial killer's victims.

JULIA SMYTHE AND DAUGHTER, PEARL SMYTHE

Holmes most certainly had a thing for women. During the course of his short life, he had countless affairs with many different women, married three of them, and would often use the appeal of engagement to lure women in as victims.

Julia Smythe was one of Holmes' mistresses. She was married while having an affair with Holmes. Her husband's name was Ned Conner. The couple had a daughter together also, Pearl.

Conner found out about what was going on between his wife and Holmes and left her and their daughter, moving to another part of the country. Smythe continued her relationship with Holmes even after her husband left. With Conner out of the picture, she wanted something more with Holmes.

Sometime after she and her daughter, Pearl, had been left behind, Smythe ended up telling Holmes she was pregnant with his baby. In 1891, she demanded that Holmes marry her. He agreed to do so, but only if she agreed to have the baby aborted. Smythe accepted his condition, agreeing to let Holmes carry out the abortion himself.

Her trust of Holmes proved to be a fatal flaw. He administered an extremely large amount of chloroform that caused her to overdose. He also poisoned Pearl and hacked her body to pieces much like a butcher does to meat.

When people took notice that the two had been missing since Christmas Eve in 1891, they started asking Holmes questions about where they'd gone. He answered them with lies about a trip to Iowa where the ladies had a family member's wedding to attend. All the while, Holmes had the bodies of both and was planning to sell them.

Holmes called on a man by the name of Charles Chappell. He wanted Chappell to help him by articulating the skeleton of Smythe so he could sell it to a school or medical lab. The man took the body to his own home to do the work Holmes had agreed to pay him for. Later on, Chappell would be hired again and again until Holmes, as he had done with the contractors that worked on his building, refused to pay Chappell for his services. At the time, Chappell still had one of the bodies at his home. He kept that skeleton, which would eventually be handed over to authorities.

EMELINE CIGRAND

There was a secretary who worked in Holmes' office. It's unclear if her relationship with her boss was more than an employer and employee, but there were rumors Holmes had, at some point, proposed to Cigrand.

Taking into consideration how Holmes had had romantic involvements with many of his victims, a reasonable person would likely conclude that he probably did have some sort of intimate relationship with his secretary.

In any case, she went missing sometime close to when Smythe and Pearl had disappeared. Her body was never found. There was a belief that some of her bones and hair had been uncovered during the search of the hotel Holmes owned. The police also interviewed a witness that claimed to have seen the janitor of the building help Holmes carry away a large chest just one day after Cigrand had gone missing.

MINNIE AND ANNIE WILLIAMS

Holmes headed to Boston to spend some time on a business trip in 1892. While in Massachusetts he met a woman named Minnie Williams. She was the heiress to a fortune her family had built working in the railroad industry. The two went on dates and spent a lot of time together during his stay in Boston. The relationship developed quickly and was deeply romantic right away.

When the trip was over, Holmes went home to Chicago to go back to work. He wrote letter after letter to Williams professing his love for her. The love notes eventually moved toward a discussion of Williams moving to Chicago to be with Holmes. He even offered her a job working as a stenographer in his new hotel that was opening to accommodate travelers coming to the city for the World's Fair.

Williams accepted the offer and moved to Chicago in early 1893. What she didn't know when she agreed to uproot herself and move in with her love was that he was digging deeper and deeper into what she had to offer him in terms of monetary gain. He found she owned property down in Fort Worth, Texas. He concocted a scheme to get his new love interest to sign the deed to the large property over to him.

Holmes told Williams of a man he knew named Alexander Bond who could help her with the management of the property. He convinced her that she needed to sign the deed over to Bond. She did just that; however, there wasn't actually an Alexander Bond at all. Bond was Holmes.

Just two months after Holmes persuaded Williams to sign the deed over to him in his devious plot, he signed the deed into the name of Benton L. Lyman. This too was part of the scheme, though. Lyman was a friend and cohort of Holmes whose real name was Benjamin Pitezel.

Pitezel and Holmes had met and become close friends back before his days as a drugstore owner and "Murder Castle" hotel entrepreneur. He had spent some time working at a bank, which is where the pair encountered each other. Holmes found Pitezel's criminal background to be intriguing and useful to himself and his endeavors.

Together, the two men would scam others out of money through insurance fraud and other kinds of crime. Pitezel was Holmes' go-to for anything he needed help with when he was scheming and defrauding people. They were less like partners in crime, though, and more like subordinates. Holmes called the shots, while Pitezel went along for the ride.

With the Fort Worth property tucked into his back pocket, Holmes took Williams to rent an apartment in the famous Lincoln Park neighborhood of the city. Williams was excited and thus invited her sister, Annie, to come and visit her in Chicago. When Annie arrived, she was quickly taken by the city lifestyle. Holmes wooed her and lured her into a close friendship almost immediately.

Annie decided to stay in Chicago for much longer than she had originally planned. She started working for Holmes in his office. One day he made a request that Annie go into his vault to find a file he needed for work. Annie entered the vault in search of the file and Holmes closed the door behind her and locked it. He then released poisonous gas into the airtight vault and asphyxiated her to death.

Holmes made quick work after that of also killing Williams. He poisoned his stenographer the same day on which he had murdered her sister, Annie.

A letter was received by the girls' aunt in July 1893. It was written as if from Annie. She was informing her aunt that she would be traveling to Europe with "Brother Harry." The aunt was not sure of what was meant by the letter, but the last time anyone ever reported having seen Annie or Williams was July 5, 1893.

There were, almost undoubtedly, many more victims. These women were just some of the most notable of his killings because, while there wasn't hard evidence proving his guilt in their murders, there were many circumstances that led many people to believe he killed them.

The World's Fair in Chicago brought millions of visitors to the city at that peak time of Holmes' murder spree. It's likely there were many killings that no one was aware of as he would trap them in his "Murder Castle," end their lives, and then dispose of the bodies in his personal incinerator in the basement of the building, or even sell them to local labs and schools.

His ability to make human remains essentially vanish coupled with his charming and beguiling personality made it easy for him to get away with many kinds of crimes.

When the World's Fair ended, Holmes had a new city on his mind's horizon. He was ready to move on and find a new hunting ground in Fort Worth.

Chapter 5

Fort Worth and St. Louis

Holmes moved around a lot during his lifetime. He frequently traveled from city to city and very likely was murdering people in these other cities along the way. But after the World's Fair was over, he wasn't just taking a trip down to Fort Worth. He decided to move there in 1893 and make use of the property he had swindled away from Minnie Williams.

"MURDER CASTLE THE SECOND"

Holmes had a plan to recreate the "Murder Castle" on the property he inherited from Williams. He needed to outrun the insurance companies that were after him for suspicion of arson, so it was a fitting time to start a new life in a new city, but not without a "playground" like he'd had for himself in Chicago.

The new castle was to be built at the corner of what is now 2nd Street and Commerce Street in Fort Worth. Plans were drawn up and Holmes hired multiple contractors just as he had the first time. Again, he didn't want any one person knowing too much about what the intended purpose of the building was.

Construction got underway, but everything was halted after Holmes, true to form, refused to pay suppliers and other contractors for their services. He abandoned his plans and "Murder Castle the Second" was never built.

MARRIED AGAIN

With his Fort Worth "Murder Castle" plans behind him, Holmes continued to travel around to different cities in the U.S. conning people along the way with the help of his dear friend Pitezel. The two made stops in places around Texas, Tennessee, Missouri, Pennsylvania, New York, and Colorado.

While in Denver, Colorado, Holmes met a woman named Georgiana Yoke. It wasn't long before an engagement came up. Then, in January 1894, he and Yoke got married. That would mean he was married to Yoke at the same time that he was Lovering and Belknap. Therefore, at this point, he had three wives.

There is belief that he may have also married Minnie Williams. By the time he married Yoke, however, Williams had already met her death at the hands of Holmes.

THE LAW CATCHES UP

Pitezel and Holmes would eventually make their way to St. Louis after the wedding with Yoke in Denver. While there, Holmes sold some items that held mortgages on them, which legally he didn't have the right to do. The police found out about the illegal sales pretty quickly, and in July 1894, they arrested him.

Holmes had spent much of his life scamming companies and people he encountered. He'd spent a lot of time murdering people, as well. This, however, would be the first time he would be incarcerated for anything.

He didn't spend a lot of time in jail, but in the short time he was there he did some talking to another inmate. The man's name was Marion Hedgepeth and he had been convicted of robbing trains. He was a career criminal who was sentenced to 25 years in jail.

Holmes told Hedgepeth about an elaborate scheme he had planned to get $10,000 out of an insurance company. In today's world that would be about the equivalent of $300,000. He said he was going to take a life insurance policy out on himself and then fake his own death.

The reason for the conversation was that Holmes needed a lawyer he could trust to draw up the policy. He offered up $500 for Hedgepeth if the convicted outlaw could provide the name of a trustworthy lawyer who would be willing to write the policy even while knowing it was for an illegal scheme. Holmes knew the scam wouldn't work if he couldn't find someone to produce the documents he needed.

Hedgepeth did cough up the name of an attorney he knew of in St. Louis who was sure to be ok with the illegal circumstances of the life insurance policy. He was a young lawyer named Jeptha Howe, and he was known by criminals to have been involved with some less than ethical characters.

Howe had a law practice where he worked alongside his older brother, Alphonso Howe. This older brother was not into any of the unscrupulous practices that the younger Howe was. He was to be left out of anything Holmes had planned.

After Holmes was bailed out of jail, he went to see Howe to take out the $10,000 life insurance policy. Howe was ok with the scam and found the plan to actually be quite brilliant. The two men worked it out where Howe would be listed as the beneficiary on the policy.

Holmes had a cadaver that he planned to use as the dead body of himself. He burned it so that no one would be able to identify the remains upon sight. Then he faked an accident in which he was caught in a fire causing his death. The insurance claim was filed after that.

It didn't go as the men had hoped, though. The insurance company decided upon investigation that the claim was invalid, thus refusing to pay out on the policy. They had been suspicious from the very beginning.

Holmes was disappointed and quite angry that his plan had not worked. He decided not to push the issue, though. The older Howe brother had not been a part in the plan at all. Holmes thought that if he pushed the claim too much, the older brother would start looking into the policy and could find evidence to have him charged and sent back to jail.

That wouldn't be the end of his idea to defraud an insurance company in this way, however. There would be another similar plan to this one in which Holmes would include his good friend Pitezel.

Chapter 6

The Pitezel Scam

Holmes wasn't going to let a failed attempt at a life insurance scam stop him from making his plans work. He quickly started working out the details of the next scheme with Pitezel and attorney Howe.

The new scam would have Pitezel at the center of it this time. In this version, he would fake his own death, allowing his wife, Carrie Pitezel, to collect the $10,000 from the life insurance policy Howe was drawing up on him. The money from Fidelity Mutual Life Association would then be split between the Pitezels, Howe, and Holmes.

There was a bit more to this plan than there had been involved in the original. Pitezel was to establish himself in Philadelphia as a man named B. F. Perry. Perry was to be an inventor who had his own laboratory and who frequently worked with combustible materials and chemicals.

As always, Holmes was to have a cadaver readily available to place in the lab as a disfigured dead version of Perry who was actually Pitezel. The scene would be set as a lab experiment that went horribly wrong with a huge explosion. The accident would take inventor Perry's life. Perry's wife, who in real life was Pitezel's wife, would file the life insurance claim and the payout would be made.

What happened next is a bit of a mystery. The actual events are clear, but the motives behind them are not. Pitezel had been Holmes' friend for quite some time. He was his right-hand man for many schemes over the course of a lot of years. It could be, though, that Holmes simply wanted more money for himself. In any case, the plan did not play out the way it was set to.

Holmes made a trip to Philadelphia. He was trying to make the new scam look as authentic as possible. He was supposed to have brought a dead body with him to place in the lab. The events that transpired after his arrival at the supposed lab of Perry would suggest that Holmes did not, in fact, have a cadaver with him as the plan had been. Maybe he had planned it that way all along or maybe he just didn't have the opportunity to acquire one, but whatever the reason was didn't matter because Holmes made the plan work anyway.

When Holmes visited the lab he ended up incapacitating Pitezel in some way. Some accounts say he knocked him out with chloroform and then set him on fire. Holmes' own account of what happened includes this order of events, though he did say Pitezel was still alive when he used benzene to set his friend on fire. It would be found later at trial that the chloroform wasn't administered until after the fire had already been set. Holmes may have been trying to make it look as if an accidental explosion in the lab had caused Pitezel to be set on fire. Then, in an attempt to stop the pain, Pitezel administered the chloroform to himself committing suicide. That would ensure that Holmes would be off the hook for the murder of his friend.

Pitezel's wife had been aware of the scam the entire time. She knew what the men were planning to do and was ok with her husband's part in the plan. Holmes communicated to her that the plan had gone off without a hitch and told her to go ahead with filing the claim.

When the insurance company investigated the accident site, they found the body of Pitezel. The authenticity provided by Holmes' killing of the actual person believed to be the inventor, Perry, paid off for Holmes. The insurance company found everything to be legit and made the determination there were grounds for a payout of the $10,000 life insurance.

Somehow, Holmes was able to convince Carrie Pitezel that her husband was still alive and in hiding so as not to interrupt the investigation or compromise the payout decision.

Holmes was the one who collected on the policy. He made sure to give Pitezel's wife $500, likely to keep her satisfied and not suspicious. The Pitezels had five children, though. And Holmes started getting paranoid that some of the kids might start suspecting something was up and eventually leak information to the police.

He appealed to their mother about taking three of the children on a trip where they could see other parts of the U.S. and some of Canada. There were two girls, Alice and Nellie, and a boy, Howard, that Carrie Pitezel unknowingly allowed into the custody of the man who had murdered her husband and their father. Two other children, the eldest girl and an infant stayed with their mother.

Holmes set off on the trip he had planned with the children. His intention was to get the kids separated from their mother so he would have the opportunity to kill them. One of the strangest parts to this segment of Holmes' story is that he was also leading Pitezel's wife along a trip route, sometimes even physically escorting her, that ran just parallel to the route he was taking the children on. She would often inquire about her husband's whereabouts and when he would be back. Holmes would always answer her questions with reassurance, telling her he went to hide in London.

Eventually, Mrs. Pitezel also started asking about where her children were. Holmes would lie to her, telling her the kids were fine and staying with various other people. He continuously assured her that they were ok and she would see them again soon. At one point on the journey in Detroit, the Pitezel children were only a few short blocks away from their mother and siblings, unbeknownst to them or Mrs. Pitezel.

While all of this was going on, Holmes' wife was none-the-wiser. She and Holmes had gotten a rental house in Toronto along the way. What she didn't know was what would eventually be found there.

Chapter 7

The Arrest of H. H. Holmes

Authorities had been starting to get very suspicious of Holmes and his ties to so many missing people. The missing Pitezel children became a big story and a police detective in Philadelphia took the case. His name was Frank Geyer.

Geyer got his investigation underway and would eventually end up in Toronto where Holmes and his unsuspecting wife had been living for a little while. He had followed the route from Philadelphia that Holmes had taken the Pitezels on during their trip.

It turned out Detective Geyer hadn't been the only one looking into Holmes. The Pinkertons were also looking for him. The

Pinkertons were a group of private detectives, led by Allan Pinkerton hired to track down wanted individuals. They had tracked Holmes when he left Philadelphia on the journey with the Pitezel children.

Holmes was eventually found by the Pinkertons in Boston with his wife. It looked as if the two were getting ready to leave the country.

The police arrested Holmes in Boston on November 17, 1894. The arrest was not for murder, however. He was charged and held for stealing horses in Texas. But, with the mounting evidence against him supporting the thoughts many had about him that he may have killed some people, the police wanted to hold on to Holmes for much more than the theft of some horses.

Even though the charges brought against Holmes were only for horse theft, he was still really upset. He feared he'd have to go back to Texas to be tried for his crime. He knew that punishments in Texas were pretty tough. So, to get out of being sent back there, Holmes admitted to the planned insurance scam he and Pitezel were in on together.

The police had an ace up their sleeve, though. They'd received a tip from that old cell mate, Hedgepeth, who'd been duped out of the money Holmes had promised him. Officers questioned Holmes about having killed Pitezel. He would not admit to killing his friend, however. Holmes changed his story several times trying to avoid a murder charge, even saying once that he'd found Pitezel's body on the floor after an apparent suicide. He claimed there had been a note with instructions to leave his portion of the insurance money to his children and to make the scene look like an accident.

Another story was that he'd had a doctor friend in New York send him a body to use for the scam. He explained that the doctor had shipped it to him in a trunk. At first, it looked like his story was going to work, but the inspector on the case had a moment of clarity. He thought back to the state of the body when it was found at the site of the staged accident. That body had been stiff with rigor mortis. That meant the person had died very recently. The inspector decided to try and back Holmes into a corner. He asked about any methods Holmes was aware of to put a body back to the state of rigor mortis once it had loosened out of it.

That did the trick. Holmes did not have an answer for the inspector's question so he was caught. There was no way the body in the lab had been that of a person dead long enough to have been shipped from New York to Philadelphia. It was determined at that point the body must have been Benjamin Pitezel.

Meanwhile, Detective Geyer's investigation was taking off. He was able to perform an inspection of the Toronto home where the

Holmes couple once lived. What he found was shocking. He uncovered the bodies of two girls that had been buried down in the cellar of the house. The bodies had been there for a while as they were badly decomposed.

Geyer's own description of what it was like when he found the girls was, "The deeper we dug, the more horrible the odor became, and when we reached the depth of three feet, we discovered what appeared to be the bone of the forearm of a human being." The police finally had irrefutable evidence against Holmes that could help prove he was a murderer.

The discovery in Toronto by Detective Geyer only included two children's bodies. Holmes' journey had included three of the Pitezel kids, though. Those were the two girls, where was the boy? Geyer's investigation wasn't finished.

Detective Geyer kept looking and going over what other stops Holmes had made since leaving Philadelphia with the children in his custody. His digging uncovered time Holmes had spent in Indianapolis. Further investigation revealed he had rented a cottage in the Indiana city. So, off to Indianapolis Geyer went.

The detective made his way around town calling on people who may have seen Holmes while he was in the city. He came across a drugstore where the pharmacist told Detective Geyer that Dr. Holmes had purchased drugs at the shop. Those drugs were later found to be what was used to kill the Pitezel boy, Howard.

Geyer knew he needed to check out the cottage Holmes had rented. Since he found the bodies of the two girls buried at Holmes' rental home in Toronto, it only made sense that there was a good chance of finding the boy's body buried at the cottage. The first search of the home and its property proved to be unsuccessful, though.

Then, Detective Geyer got a tip from the owner of a repair shop in town. Geyer heard about Holmes visiting the repair shop with some knives he owned. He went there to have them sharpened. That information meant that maybe he shouldn't be looking for a whole body.

Armed with what he found out, Geyer went back to the cottage for another search. In a second search of the home, the detective was able to recover some human teeth and pieces of bones. They were found in the chimney.

In the end, it was determined that the teeth and bone fragments were that of Howard Pitezel. Holmes had killed the boy with drugs from the pharmacy. He then chopped up the body and burned it in the fireplace of the cottage. While his plan was to dispose of the boy's remains so he wouldn't be found out, he wasn't quite able to destroy all of the evidence completely.

Geyer knew what his next step had to be. He went to track down Dr. Holmes.

Of course Holmes was already in custody. The longer he was in jail, the more he started talking about some of the things he had done. He explained how he had killed the two Pitezel girls. He said he put Nellie and Alice inside a large trunk alive. He locked them in. Then he made a small hole in the lid just big enough to get a hose through. He used the hose to pump gas through that killed the girls.

After the girls were dead, he took them out of the trunk. He removed and disposed of their clothing. Then he carried them down to the cellar of the rental house he lived in with Yoke in Toronto and buried them in the spot where Detective Geyer had found them.

During the time he was held in jail, which was almost a year before his trial, police were looking into more and more of their suspicions surrounding Holmes' activities. The Chicago Police Department went to the "Murder Castle" in Englewood to search the building to see what they could turn up. Their search didn't reveal anything that could really be used as substantial evidence to convict Holmes of murder.

This is one area where there are many differences of opinion and belief. Looking at the printed articles in the *New York Times* at that time, there are reports stating, "…persons have been cruelly murdered in this chamber of horrors…" in reference to Holmes' Englewood building. Many stories were printed in various publications with descriptions of all of the torture devices, medical implements, and other oddities that were found in Holmes' building.

Stories were released about the staircases heading to nowhere, rooms that locked only from the outside, rooms with no windows, and oddly shaped hallways. The problem is that there are also accounts of a building that may have had some strange architectural features, but did not, in fact, have anything close to torture devices and the like.

The media outlets of that time were known to often embellish stories at fantastic proportions. There was always a push to shock the audience so readers would keep coming back for more. Exaggeration of stories was the norm at the time.

Either way, whether the "Murder Castle" was full of secret passages, airtight rooms, and other implements that could be used to kill people, or it just simply had some eerie features that people weren't used to seeing in a typical building, it was, with almost certainty, the murder scene for several of Holmes' victims.

By this point, there was plenty of other evidence to use in an attempt to convict Holmes and keep him from ever killing again.

Chapter 8

The End of
the H. H. Holmes Era

By the fall of 1895, bodies and pieces of bodies had been popping up in various places with plenty of reasons for thinking Holmes was to blame for the deaths of all of them. Authorities were ready to put the killer away for good.

Police didn't think they had enough evidence to officially charge Holmes with all of the murders they believed he had committed. But, they did charge him with the murder of his cohort, Ben Pitezel.

Even though the inspector had caught him in a lie, Holmes tried to maintain his innocence regarding the death of Pitezel. He continued to try to convince his captors that the body they had found at the lab accident site was not that of his friend. He made multiple references to the insurance scam they had worked out before all of that took place. And he continued to push that Pitezel was simply in hiding.

Eventually he would start to change his story, however. Rather than accept responsibility for killing any of his victims, Holmes made confessions to killing people with his own actions but at the beckoning of the devil.

He was quoted as saying, "I was born with the devil in me. I could not help the fact that I was a murderer, no more than the poet can help the inspiration to sing – I was born with the 'Evil One' standing as my sponsor beside the bed where I was ushered into the world, and he has been with me since."

The trial ended with a guilty verdict. Holmes was convicted of the murder of Benjamin Pitezel. His sentence was death by hanging.

After the conviction, Holmes started making confessions. He told police that he actually killed 27 people. Of course three of those were Alice, Nellie, and Howard Pitezel. The others he said were people he killed in Toronto, Chicago, and Indianapolis. He also confessed that he'd tried to kill six people that had gotten away.

[51]

When police started looking into the murders of the people Holmes had included in his confession, they discovered some baffling things. Some of the supposed victims Holmes said he'd killed were actually still very much alive and well. They didn't know what to make of his false confessions.

To this day, all of the fraud, conning, lying, and changes of his stories have made it very difficult for anyone to know exactly how many lives this serial killer may have taken.

What's more intriguing is the fact that Holmes even sold his story to Hearst newspapers. They paid him $7,500 so he would tell them everything he'd done. But, as most of what he said was made up, it didn't help at all in figuring out what the truth was.

One school of thought regards Holmes as truly a psychopath. There was no diagnosis for that at the time, however. Holmes may very well have believed the devil was in control of what he was doing. He even wrote about his Satanic possession from jail when he was putting the details of his story down on paper for Hearst. He said in the writings that he was starting to look very much like the devil. His description of himself mentioned "gruesome," and he seemed to believe that Satan was not just inside his body but that he, Holmes, was actually becoming the devil.

THE HANGING

Holmes' hanging was scheduled for May 7, 1896. Though he knew he was going to be killed, he maintained his poise and calm demeanor all the way through his time in prison. He was to be hanged at the Philadelphia County Prison.

Leading up to his hanging, Holmes expressed that he would like his coffin to be encased in cement. He also wanted to be buried 10 feet down. His fear was that grave robbers would exhume his body and sell it to a medical research lab or school to be dissected. He didn't want what he did to his victims to happen to him.

On the day of the hanging, Holmes was escorted up to the gallows. He was prepared for his punishment by the prison's authorities. While standing on the platform before being hanged, it's been said Holmes changed his story one last time, stating he only actually ever killed two people, and that those were accidental while performing abortions. As his conviction had already been issued, this new confession had no meaningful effect, except to add more confusion to an already muddled story.

When the time came, the question was asked, "Ready, Dr. Holmes?" His response was "Yes. Don't bungle." At that, the platform was dropped, but the force of the fall was not enough to break Holmes' neck as it was supposed to. His fate was much worse.

His body hung from the gallows for more than 15 minutes while he struggled for air. He died a slow and agonizing death by strangulation rather than the quick execution it was intended to be.

END OF STORY?

Not quite. This is a story about a fraudster and killer where the con seemed to continue even after his death.

The rumor mill started up and people were talking about Holmes having escaped his execution. The chatter stemmed from an article printed in the newspaper about a bribe carried out by Holmes in prison. The story was that he had convinced a jailer to put him in a coffin and carry it out of the jail. He'd allegedly run away after that, never to be seen again. It was thought he'd fled to Paraguay where he was living as a coffee grower because that's what Holmes' janitor alleged. Further claims were that it wasn't actually him that was buried in the grave marked with his name near Philadelphia. People said it was a cadaver Holmes had in his possession just like he'd used in so many of his other scams.

Historians from then until now have been trying to piece together the facts surrounding H. H. Holmes for more than a century. Some of what they'd like to prove there is just no plausible way of doing so. Confirming the identity of who was or was not buried in Holmes' grave, however, was something they did have the ability to do. So they did.

At the beckoning of some of Holmes' descendants, great-grandchildren, John Mudgett, Richard Mudgett, and Cynthia Mudgett Soriano, Janet Monge and a team from the University of Pennsylvania Museum of Archaeology and Anthropology exhumed the body that was buried in the grave labeled as Holmes in 2017. What they found was a male body that hadn't decomposed to the degree that would normally be seen after such a long time. The clothes Holmes had worn when he was hanged were in almost perfect condition. His mustache looked just as it had in life.

The team ran tests on the teeth, as would be performed on unidentified bodies in any present day case, also. The tests confirmed that the body was indeed that of H. H. Holmes, a.k.a. Herman Webster Mudgett. With the confirmation made, the body was then reburied as it had been found.

Holmes had fathered two children, one with each of two of his wives. He had a son with Clara Lovering, Robert Lovering Mudgett, and a daughter with Myrta Belknap, Lucy Theodate Holmes. Both of the kids lived long productive lives.

Robert completed college and became a certified public accountant. He eventually moved to Florida, established a family, and spent time as the city manager of Orlando. He had two children of his own with his wife, Alexandra Gilbert. He died at the age of 76 in New Smyrna, Florida.

After her dad's conviction and writing him a long heartfelt letter saying goodbye, Lucy moved with her mom to Minnesota, where both women found jobs in the school system. Later, Lucy took a position as the secretary for her local branch of the Red Cross. She was involved in teaching in France during WWI, which is where she met her first husband. The couple returned to the states and were together until things fell apart about four years into the marriage. She married again, but that union didn't last long either. Though they were separated, Lucy asserted she was still married all the way through her death in 1956. She was 67 years old.

Chapter 9

Methods of a Serial Killer

Serial killers are people who kill more than one victim in separate incidents. For the most part, they will have murdered three or more people. But there are some instances in which someone has been deemed a serial killer who has killed just two people on separate occasions.

Typically, there are long periods of time between the incidents. It's also something that usually goes on until someone or something causes the killer to stop. The person either dies or is caught and locked away.

Motivation for a serial killer is often tied to satisfying an inner psychological need. There is a gratification that is obtained as a result of the killings. Other motives have been identified as well, such as gaining attention, the thrill of the kill, anger, and financial gain.

One thing most serial killers have in common is they use the same or similar method of killing their victims each time. Some of them even have what many law enforcement agencies refer to as a "calling card." It's essentially a signature left behind at the crime scene that shows ownership of the murder. The killer is saying, "Look what I did." This is often seen with serial killers who are motivated by seeking attention.

H. H. Holmes was an atypical serial killer in that he didn't always use the same method to kill his victims. In his case, there were reportedly several different ways he killed people. While many serial killers also kill similar types of people, Holmes also strayed away from the norm on that front, too. He likely killed more women than men, but his victims included women, men, and children.

Holmes mostly targeted his lovers, his employees, and guests staying at his hotel. There were various reasons for him having killed specific people, but the underlying factor that seemed to run through most of his murders, as well as many other kinds of his scams, was some sort of financial windfall he would receive after the targeted person was dead or the scheme played out. There seemed to be a greed that existed within him, driving him to make more and more money at any cost—the cost being, many times, someone's life.

The thing about Holmes was that he didn't always kill people in the same way. The murders he's believed to be responsible for took place in different ways.

Asphyxiation does seem to have been a method he enjoyed using. The famed "Murder Castle" he had built was said to have had airtight and soundproofed rooms where he would lock people in and then pump gas into them, killing the person inside. The two Pitezel girls he is known to have killed were asphyxiated inside the trunk, as Holmes himself admitted.

There are also accounts of a "Secret Hanging Chamber" that existed inside Holmes' building. Several lengths of rope had been found during searches of the property, as well. Some of the victims were believed to have been hanged at the "Murder Castle."

Still others were trapped inside the airtight vault Holmes had in the building. They would be left in there to die of suffocation.

One of the cruelest accounts of his probable murders included the use of a bricked up room. There was no true door to the room, only a trapdoor in the ceiling that the person inside wouldn't be able to reach. It's believed Holmes would trap victims in the secret brick room and leave them there as long as it took for them to starve to death or die of dehydration.

Holmes wrote about a man he had attempted to kill by starvation. At the time, Holmes had been writing confessions to various news publications to get his story out in the public while he was sitting in prison waiting for his hanging day. In his letter to one of the media outlets he stated that though he was trying to starve the man, he killed him in some other unspecified fashion because he needed that space, "for another purpose and because his pleadings had become almost unbearable…"

His other methods included poisoning people, overdosing them on chloroform, burning victims, and he said he even hired a man to commit one murder for him.

Once the person was dead, Holmes typically would take one of two routes. He would either prepare the body to be sold to a medical research lab or a school, or he would destroy it so there wouldn't be evidence to incriminate him.

Many of the corpses were used to make money for Holmes. The "Murder Castle" had an incinerator in the basement, along with medical tables and tools, and chutes located all throughout the building that led down to that basement. The bodies he planned to sell were put into a chute and sent down to where they could be prepared properly. Holmes would then have to dissect the body completely and remove all of the flesh from the bones. After that, the bones would be pieced back together into a skeleton that could be sold to schools in the area. Prior to doing it himself, he had his accomplice, Chappell, do it, until their falling out over payment.

It's hard to say if H. H. Holmes had a preferred method of killing. He seemed to vary his practices, but usually repeated most methods that worked for him previously. Also, the fact that there's not a perfectly clear picture of exactly how many victims there were whom had been killed by Holmes makes it hard to know with certainty some of the details about this serial killer.

What is known about him is fascinating. He seems, by all accounts, to have kept people guessing throughout his entire living existence. And even in death, more than a century later, he still has people wondering and trying to figure out who Dr. H. H. Holmes truly was.

Chapter 10

Was H. H. Holmes the Infamous "Jack the Ripper?"

In 1888, an unidentified killer was roaming the streets of London in the Whitechapel district kidnapping and murdering women working as prostitutes. All of the bodies police discovered had been brutally mutilated in a meticulous fashion, as if by the hand of a skilled doctor. There were five known victims in total.

"Jack the Ripper" was the name given to the unknown killer. It was inspired by the state of the bodies that were found. They had been disfigured in specific regions of the body in a highly unusual fashion. The killer was never identified, however, there are several working theories for who the man could have been.

Flash forward to the 21st century and a lawyer named Jeff Mudgett believes he has the answer to the question of who "Jack the Ripper" was. Mudgett, who was once a Commander in the United States Naval Reserve, is the great-great-grandson of H. H. Holmes, or Herman Webster Mudgett.

Mudgett's beliefs originally stemmed from a couple of diaries he was given that had been handed down through his family. He found pages of writings about murders that included mutilation of prostitutes in London. The diary entries indicated in detail that Holmes had participated in those murders.

There's certainly the possibility that Holmes was also London's "Jack the Ripper," however, he proved on countless occasions his propensity for lying. He made several confessions of murders, only to change them later to something completely different. He took responsibility for killing people who were found to be alive and well. Could Holmes have lied about murdering prostitutes in London in his diary? Yes, of course he could have. But, he also could have been telling the truth.

Mudgett decided to take the investigation into his great-great-grandfather to the next level to see if he could connect all of the dots between Holmes and the unknown killer in London, proving they were one in the same. He brought on a former CIA agent named Amaryllis Fox to help him figure things out.

The pair looked at both angles—they were the same person or they were separate people who just happened to be killing people on opposite sides of an ocean around the same time. Their goal was to compare any similarities, as well as any differences, and see if a determination could be made.

THE DIFFERENCES

There were certainly some differences between what happened in London and what had happened in parts of the U.S. First, there's the M.O., or modus operandi, to look at. "Jack the Ripper" killed his victims out in the streets of Whitechapel where he could have been discovered by any passersby. Holmes killed people behind closed doors, or walls, in some cases. He even built himself a private "killer's playground" of sorts.

Geography certainly plays a huge role in the differences for these killers. Their murders took place on completely separate continents. So separate, in fact, there is an entire ocean between them. Mudgett and Fox tried to find some sort of evidence that Holmes traveled to England in 1888, but there was nothing with enough strength behind it to be called proof.

A note about that time, though, that's worth mentioning, is this investigation did uncover a paper trail that allowed the pair to track Holmes' movements over the course of much of his life. The trail goes cold during part of 1888 through part of 1889, though, right when the London murders were taking place. Most have chocked that off to mere coincidence, but it does beg the question, where was Holmes located during that break in the documentation trail? There was a ship log discovered from the timeframe just after the London killings had ended. A passenger named H. Holmes was indicated to have been on it traveling back to the U.S. from the UK, but there's been no way to prove that was the same Holmes.

There seems to be an evident difference in the motives of these two killers. Holmes didn't appear to murder people for the sheer high of killing someone. It also didn't seem like he liked attention. In fact, it was quite the opposite with him. "Jack the Ripper," on the other hand seemed mainly motivated by a need to satisfy some deep craving just to kill. There was no financial gain in it for him and he, very much, appeared to want some kind of attention.

THE SIMILARITIES

There are some details that seem to parallel each other between these two murderers. The victims in London had all been choked first, either to death or to a point of passing out. Their killer would then lay them on the ground in the street where he encountered them. Then, he methodically eviscerated their bodies with a knife, removing parts of the body with precision. He was never caught because he made sure the women could not scream or yell for help. The whole encounter was completed very quietly.

The disfigurement of the bodies was done in such a way that people speculated the killer had to have had some sort of medical training. Holmes went to medical school and also used those learned skills and abilities in his killings. Both of these murderers are believed to have medical training.

"Jack the Ripper" was credited with one murder that was different than all of his others. He had killed five women outside in the streets of London. What's believed to be his last victim, however, was found dead in her own home on her bed. The mutilation done to her body was much different than that of the other victims, also. The others had been precisely cut open and parts of their bodies removed quite carefully. This body had been absolutely obliterated. The killer had slashed her up so much, it would have been almost impossible to identify her had she not been found in her own bed.

Mudgett and Fox had a theory about that last murder in London. Their thoughts were that it could have been Holmes' intention to try out a different style of killing before returning to the U.S. and going on the hunt for more victims.

Those who have studied "Jack the Ripper" are all familiar with what has been deemed the "Dear Boss" letter. The letter was supposedly written by the London killer and sent to media agencies around the city at the time of the murders. Upon analysis of the language used in the letter, some experts believe the letter was written by an American.

One of the most convincing pieces in the puzzle of whether Holmes was, in fact, the same killer dubbed "Jack the Ripper" who was killing prostitutes in London, came in the form of eyewitness descriptions. There had been a man people had been noticing who was seen with the murdered women before they went missing. In total, 13 witnesses described a man in much the same way. Those descriptions were given to a modern-day forensic sketch artist by Mudgett and Fox. The picture of the killer that took shape looked eerily very much like portraits of Holmes. Mudgett believed the sketch resembled Holmes so much, that if they were looking for the killer today, it would be enough to get an arrest warrant issued.

Not Enough

Though there's been a lot of investigation into this matter, the jury is still out on if Holmes was indeed "Jack the Ripper." Those interested in the case can find an eight-episode series that aired on a popular tv channel available for streaming online. It follows the investigation that Mudgett and Fox conducted, revealing all the connections they found between the two.

Others have also been suspected to have been responsible for the London murders, but the Mudgett theory had certainly proven to be one of the strongest. That was, until in 2019 news broke that there had been DNA found on a possible piece of evidence that was tested. The results came back with the name of one of the other men who'd been a suspect at one point. The man's name was Aaron Kosminski. His semen had been present on a shawl that had been found close to the fourth victim's body. Modern technology allowed researchers to identify whose it was.

The bottom line is there just isn't enough actual evidence to say which suspect, if any of them, was the actual man behind the "Jack the Ripper" murders. There is a lot of circumstantial evidence that can be pointed to in support of Mudgett's theory. At this point, it's up to each on their own to decide what to believe.

Chapter 11

He Lives On

Plenty of people, including writers, poets, filmmakers, and journalists have decided what they believe, or in the very least have tried to figure out what they believe regarding this serial killer. This story of H. H. Holmes has been retold numerous times over the years in many interesting ways. The mystery and intrigue of it all has withstood the test of time and made it to the forefront of pop culture for generation after generation to explore.

The case was already popular back in the time when the killings were taking place. Several publications were releasing articles about Holmes and his "Murder Castle" even before he was convicted. *The New York Times* printed a whole series of stories about it.

Then, after his arrest and conviction, Holmes spent his time writing letters to multiple newspapers telling several versions of the "truth," some of which were contradictory to each other. There was widespread interest in the story, even back then.

To this day, interest hasn't faded. Hollywood director Martin Scorsese started work in 2019 on a new filmed version of the Holmes story, *The Devil in the White City.* Famed actor Leonardo DiCaprio is partnering with Scorsese to bring the 2003 book by Erik Larson to the masses. DiCaprio stars as the main character, playing Dr. H. H. Holmes, himself.

Going back over the decades, there are many other publicized versions of the Holmes case. In 1940, Herbert Asbury's book titled *Gem of the Prairie: An Informal History of the Chicago Underworld* included a chapter called "The Monster of Sixty-Third Street" about Holmes and his huge building in Englewood. It saw a second publishing in 1986, as well.

Holmes' life was the inspiration for the fictional story in *American Gothic.* This was a novel written by Robert Bloch in 1974. The main character in the psychological horror book was given a different name, G. Gordon Gregg.

A book by David Franke in 1975 was called *The Torture Doctor.* It told the story of notorious Dr. H. H. Holmes for the new generation to read. It's an easy read and good introduction into the life of the nation's first known serial killer.

In 1985, a novel was written about Holmes, which pays much attention to the "Murder Castle" he had built in Chicago. It details some of the murders, as well as the chase by Detective Geyer who was assigned to work the Holmes case after suspicions started getting stronger that the doctor had something to do with the disappearance of the Pitezel children and the death of their father. This book, too, has seen a second publishing in 2000.

Author Harold Schechter wrote a nonfictional account of Holmes' story in 1994. The book covers the life of Holmes, trying to figure out how many murders there were. It's called *Depraved: The Shocking True Story of America's First Serial Killer* and was one of many stories Schechter wrote about serial killers.

In 2003 was when Erik Larson released his hugely popular book, *The Devil in the White City: Murder, Magic, and Madness at the Fair That Changed America.* This book really brought a lot of attention back to the story of Holmes. There was a renewed surge of interest in this mysterious serial killer's case. Seven years after the book's release, Leonardo DiCaprio bought the rights to the book's story with intentions to turn the book into a feature film.

A popular television show, "Supernatural," created by Eric Kripke, featured fictional stories based on dark fantasy ideas. The two main characters are brothers who spend their days and nights hunting down monsters, demons, ghosts, and other supernatural entities. In an episode titled "No Exit" that aired in 2006, the brothers are tracking a ghost. The antagonist ghost is that of the serial killer, H. H. Holmes.

The most recent versions of Holmes' story came in 2017, when a biography by Adam Selzer called *H. H. Holmes: The True History of the White City Devil* was published. It chronicles the murders that took place within Holmes' hotel during the World's Fair in Chicago. This book takes a deep dive into paperwork found, letters written, and all other evidence available for analysis surrounding the Holmes case. It reviews the story in detail, but also looks at how certain aspects of the case have evolved through time. Selzer's goal was to reveal any untruths that have been passed down about the case to uncover what the real facts of the story are.

There was also a documentary series aired on the HISTORY channel in the second half of 2017. That series, "American Ripper," was the series mentioned earlier which follows Holmes' great-great-grandson, Jeff Mudgett, as he tries to figure out just who his great-great-grandfather was, and if he was the man behind the "Jack the Ripper" killings in London during 1888. In it, Mudgett pairs up with ex-CIA operative Amaryllis Fox to see how far they can get with connecting the dots between the two late 19th century murderers. Though it aired a few years back, the eight episodes can still be accessed through streaming services today.

Prior to the "American Ripper" series, Mudgett had written a book called *Bloodstains*. This is the written version of what inspired the HISTORY channel nonfiction series. The documentary video series takes viewers through the story of Holmes and weighs the evidence in support of, and against, the notion that Holmes is also "Jack the Ripper." *Bloodstains,* however, tells everything in much more detail. The book is nonfiction, but some of the story is so convoluted and twisted, it feels like a psychological thriller novel with a pull toward the paranormal.

Another recent publication won the Bram Stoker Award for Best Poetry Collection in 2018. It's a collection of poems by Sara Tantlinger, an accomplished horror writer, entitled *The Devil's Dreamland: Poetry Inspired by H. H. Holmes.*

Scorsese and DiCaprio eventually struck a deal with Hulu that included turning the Larson book into a television series, rather than a movie. Alongside the main character of Holmes, there will also be a character by the name of Daniel H. Burnham. Burnham was a brilliant architect in the late 19th century and early 20th century. The series will follow the tales of both serial killer and architect, telling their stories, including those of the construction of the "Murder Castle" and the murders that took place within it.

Conclusion

Notoriety for
a Century and Beyond

H. H. Holmes was America's first known and dubbed serial killer. His life was one of constant scheming to make more money. He lied, stole, cheated, defrauded, and killed to get what he was after.

Early on, there had been signs of extreme intelligence of the boy, but also of abnormal behaviors, like an obsessive interest in the anatomy of the human body and a need to dissect helpless animals. He was also very strongly drawn to the medical field and eventually enrolled in medical school.

Many of the details about Holmes' life may have been lost through the years, but the big picture can still be seen. He was a greedy man who would stop at nothing to build his fortune. He did a lot of traveling and swindled people he met along the way. He also, very likely murdered some he encountered on his trips.

Holmes was apprehended because there was a warrant out for his arrest after he had stolen a horse in Texas. After some digging, police were only able to charge him with the murder of one man, his one-time friend, Ben Pitezel. They didn't need any more than that, though, because he was tried and convicted, then sentenced to death.

He made many confessions after being caught to killing many more people than authorities knew about. With every confession, the story became more and more twisted. It's unknown if Holmes was a psychopath who truly didn't have the capacity to know what the truth was, or if he took pleasure in the confusion he caused with his contradicting stories, almost as if he was playing a game.

Overall, there's been solid connections made between Holmes and the murders of 10 people. The facts surrounding this serial killer are so convoluted, though, the world will likely never know the true number of people he murdered in his quest for money. There's no doubt, though, that some will press forward, continuing to seek the truth about the notorious serial killings of H. H. Holmes.

Pop culture shows proof of the everlasting interest and the intriguing nature of this life story. Holmes was a serial killer who often left a trail of fraud, questions, and havoc in his wake. He was dangerous, intelligent, devious, and self-serving. But eventually, it was a horse and a friend that brought America's first notorious serial killer down. Holmes' murder spree ended when he was just 34 years old.

Printed in Great Britain
by Amazon